KAREL HUSA

SONATINA

for Piano

Associated Music Publishers, Inc.

DISTRIBUTED BY

HAL•LEONARD®
CORPORATION
7777 W. BLUEMOUND RD. P.O. BOX 13819 MILWAUKEE, WI 53213

SONATINA
for Piano

KAREL HUSA
(1943)

Allegretto moderato

Allegretto marciale

0-73999-67270-1

HL50226530

U.S. $19.99

ISBN 978-0-634-04824-1

51999

Associated Music Publishers, Inc.

DISTRIBUTED BY